THE BEST 50

SUSHI ROLLS

Carol M. Newman

BRISTOL PUBLISHING ENTERPRISES
San Leandro, California

Printed in the United States of America.

ISBN 1-55867-211-7
Cover design: Frank J. Paredes
Cover photography: John A. Benson
Food styling: Carol M. Newman

SUSHI – LET IT ROLL

The Japanese lifestyle is admired for its minimalist, streamlined simplicity. This living structure is, no doubt, carried over into Japanese culinary formalities. On the surface, the well-designed sushi one orders or visualizes appears to be complex. And at first glance, these tightly-wrapped petite structures may appear intimidating. But elegance does not always mean complex. Rather, it is the natural result when one emphasizes refined, simple and fresh.

Generally, there are very few ingredients in a given Japanese sushi item. But what gives these special pieces their character is that the ingredients are incredibly fresh and pleasing to the eye, mind and palate. For the Japanese, refinement in all things – taste, size, smell, or texture outweighs a melange of mismatched traits.

Unfortunately, narrow assumptions often box in Japanese cuisine. Sushi is misunderstood as being "too expensive" and/or "all about fish." Whereas "sashimi" purely defines raw fish, the definition for "sushi" is a little more slippery. Sushi refers to rolls

made with or without fish and with vegetables or other fillings. Rice, however, must be included in the roll in order to be called sushi. And so we get the roll–inside-out, or temaki, a cone-shaped hand roll that is the size of an ice cream cone. Maki is usually served in six slices and is made with seaweed. Nigiri, or hand-made sushi, is typically ordered and served in pairs. There is also pressed sushi or oshi, which is cut into small squares. This book focuses only on maki, rolled with the rice on the inside or outside of the roll.

SOUNDS FISHY

A rather stiff myth is that eating sushi is a cause for alarm – that raw fish is in some way a danger. This needs explanation. There are some fish that are considered safer to eat raw than others. Saltwater fish, however, such as tuna, halibut, salmon and shellfish are safe to eat raw if caught in nonpolluted waters. "Sashimi-grade" fish is of a higher quality and is more expensive. The higher the fat content of a fish, the more flavor it will have. So, keep this in mind

when you shop for tuna or salmon. If you are still hesitant about eating raw fish, double check with your fish purveyor. Let him/her know you are planning to make sushi and seek their advice on quality and freshness. The general rule for freshness is this: make sure the fish smells like the ocean, rather than ammonia. You'll want to make sure the eyes are clear (if buying a whole fish), rather than dull, that the flesh bounces back when poked and that there are no signs of browning. Freshwater fish from lakes and streams should never be used for sushi. If you plan on using a fresh water fish, cooking it thoroughly is resistance against parasites. If you are still squeamish, use the recipes in this book that call for cooked fish, canned fish or produce.

LET IT ROLL BABY, ROLL

Learn to roll sushi and you will not only add a culinary skill to your repertoire, but you will be able to share in a Japanese custom from the 1800s, and in the Western world, that of the Edo tradition, or, sushi formed by hand. For hundreds of years, the Japanese

preserved their fish with salt and pressed it in layers until the fish was fermented. In the early 1800s, a Japanese entrepreneur decided to put raw seafood on pads of rice. The new trend emerged and quickly caught on throughout Japan and the rest of the world.

EQUIPMENT

A quick word about equipment. You can do a lot with very little. There are no fancy gadgets involved. If you have the basics and some skill, you are on the way to becoming a sushi aficionado. When you do reach that level, think about investing in some sake cups, your own special chopsticks and some real Japanese dishware. In the meantime, pick up these few items:

• A bamboo mat or hot pad, called a sushimaki sudare or a *makisu*. This is used to roll the sushi.

• A wooden rice paddle, or a *shamoji*. This is used to "cut" the rice after cooking and spread it on the nori.

• A very sharp knife is a must. The classic sushi knife is called a *bento knife*.

• Chopsticks are called *hashi*; learn to use them like a pro.

THE LUCK OF THE ROLL (ROLLING METHOD)

Lay your sushi mat flat on the counter and cover with plastic wrap. Take a piece of sushi nori and lay it glossy-side down. Wet your hands and scoop ½ cup cooked rice out of the bowl. Make a thin, loose "line" of rice across the seaweed. Wet hands again and gently massage rice so that you distribute rice into a thin sheet. The grains should be kept intact. Fill your roll in layers, trying to use long pieces of whatever filling you are going to roll. Using the bamboo mat to guide you, take the edge nearest you and curl it over (as you would a sleeping bag), tuck the edge in as tightly as you can and begin to roll. You may have to use your finger to keep the filling from popping out. DO NOT ROLL THE BAMBOO MAT INTO YOUR ROLL. Seal with a swipe of water. Finally, using a VERY sharp, clean

knife, cut the ends to make even. When slicing the roll, cut straight through very quickly. Next, cut the roll in half and put the two identical shorter rolls next to each other. Cut these pieces until there are six equal pieces of sushi.

INSIDE-OUT

You can also try wrapping your rolls inside-out. Flip the nori sheet over after you massage the rice, and place the fillings on the other side of the nori, layering them as you would with the regular roll. Follow the same rolling procedure on previous page. Cut into six equal slices with a clean, sharp knife.

INSIDE THE SUSHI KITCHEN

avocado: make sure it is ripe and dark-skinned.

daikon: radish

gari or shoga: sliced, pickled ginger, a condiment used to reset the palate and tastebuds.

imitation crab: look for this if you can't find the
real thing

kappa: cucumber. European cucumbers are recommended
because there is less waste.

kuro goma: sesame seeds, available in black or white

nori: toasted seaweed sheets. Look for the dark green color with
a high glossy finish.

shoyu: the fermented soy bean sauce or soy sauce comes in different styles. Japanese soy has a relatively sweet flavor and is less
salty than Chinese or American varieties.

su or awaze-zu: sushi vinegar. Fermented rice wine or rice
vinegar.

sushi rice: look for Kokuho Rose or Nishiki brands. Do not use
sweet rice. The grains of sushi rice are small and fat. The rice
tends to be starchy, rinse it well.

plum sauce: a thick sauce made from apricots, chiles, vinegar and sugar

wasabi: green horseradish paste that either comes in dry form or in small cans. It comes in varying degrees of "heat". Wasabi is a perennial plant and, as it ages, a rhizome forms. That is the most valued part of the plant. Fresh wasabi is premium, and if you can find it, use it. Unfortunately, many restaurants and food markets carry green food-colored horseradish.

A FEW POLITE JAPANESE PHRASES THAT MAY HELP YOUR POPULARITY WHEN YOU VISIT A SUSHI BAR

Arigato: thank you. Be nice; use it often.

Arigato gozaimashita: Final thank you at the end of the meal

Itamae-san: the sushi chef. These chefs 'conduct' the sushi bar as a conductor conducts an orchestra. By just glancing at your plate, a good Itamae san will pin your sushi tastes down. He may make suggestions. A sushi chef is involved in every detail of the preparation, from haggling with fish and produce purveyors, to preparing the sushi and being the master showman behind the sushi bar. Show plenty of respect for your Itamae-san.

Kanapi: the Japanese equivalent of "cheers," used when drinking

Konbonwa: good evening

O kudasai: please give me. First, say the type of sushi you want then, "o kudasai." Example: "Tekka-maki o kudasai" means "Please give me a tuna roll."

Oma ka se: chef's choice. This is a magic word with your itamae san. It tells the chef to make whatever he wants. It is considered a great honor. Use it to your advantage (you may receive extra sushi – gratis!)

Oshibori: hot towel to wipe your face and hands before you eat

Oyasumi nasai: good night

SUSHI – LET IT ROLL

DO'S AND DON'TS AT THE SUSHI BAR

Here are a few words of etiquette to keep in mind. Know the Japanese traditions and try them. But within the restraints of common law and courtesy, enjoy your meal however you like!

1. Use the hot towel that is given to you at the sushi bar to clean your hands and your face before a meal.

2. Avoid drinking sake with sushi. Because sake is made with rice, it is redundant for the Japanese to have both in the same sitting. Example: Serving baked potatoes with a side of French fries.

3. Avoid using wasabi (even though they give it to you) with your sushi. The itamae-san sometimes puts wasabi in your sushi, between the rice and fish. Adding wasabi is to tell the itamae-san he did not season the sushi properly. (Example: Adding salt to a plate you have not tasted yet with the cook sitting beside you).

4. It's okay to eat sushi with your fingers. When you dip your sushi in soy sauce, try not to let any grains fall into the soy and be

careful about how much you get on your rice; the sushi roll could fall apart. If the roll is too big for one bite, bite it in half, but NEVER PUT IT BACK ON YOUR PLATE, HALF-EATEN; this is not appropriate.

5. If you decide to sample sushi from a friend's plate with your chopsticks, turn them around and use the back end.

6. If your sushi chef is doing a nice job for you, offer to buy him a drink, maybe a sake or beer. This is a nice thing to do and it may help build your relationship.

7. Like Mom used to say, finish your food! In Japan, it is an insult to leave food on your plate.

8. When you are finished eating, align your chopsticks neatly on the edge of your plate. Do not haphazardly lie them down in the soy or on your placemat.

SUSHI RICE

This is the recipe you will use to make all of the sushi recipes in this book. The recipe makes 4 sushi rolls or 24 pieces of maki. The rice tastes best when it is a little crunchy; this will help keep the grains intact.

2 cups short-grain rice (Kokuho Rose or Nishiki)
2 cups water
1/4 cup rice vinegar
3 tbs. sugar
1 tsp. salt

Wash rice until water runs clear; drain in a colander. Transfer rice to a pot or electric rice cooker and add water. Bring water to a boil. Simmer over low heat, allowing rice to steam for 15 minutes with the cover on at all times. Remove from heat and keep covered, allowing to steam for 15 minutes. Mix rice vinegar, sugar and salt. With a wooden spoon, fold vinegar mixture into rice; avoid smashing grains. Spread rice on baking pan to cool. Makes 4 cups.

SHRIMP TEMPURA
ROLL (EBI)

*Tempura means battered and lightly fried. It a favorite Japanese
cooking method, and popular with the less daring sushi fanatics.*

6 black tiger shrimp, peeled and deveined
1/4 cup all-purpose flour, plus more for dredging
1/2 tsp. cornstarch
1 egg
1/2 cup ice water
canola oil, for deep frying
2 sheets sushi nori
2 green onions, ends trimmed
1 cup cooked sushi rice, page 13

In a small bowl, mix flour, cornstarch, egg and ice water. Sprinkle extra flour on a plate. Score shrimp across backs and press down to elongate. Heat oil over high heat, checking temperature by dropping a spoonful of batter in oil. The temperature is right if the piece drops halfway and then floats back to the surface. Batter shrimp, dredge in flour and fry until golden brown. Drain on paper towels.

Heat nori in a 350° oven to soften slightly, about 3 to 4 minutes. Working with one sheet of nori at a time, with shiny side facing down and with long side facing you, spread ½ cup of the rice in an even layer on each sheet, leaving a ½-inch border on long sides. Arrange shrimp in a line across rice. Arrange a green onion on top of shrimp. Follow rolling procedure on page 5 and cut each roll into 6 equal slices. Makes 12 slices.

Variation

Vegetable Tempura Roll: Batter and fry assorted chopped vegetables, such as broccoli.

THE CALIFORNIA ROLL

A Western tradition, this little gem has made its way onto virtually every sushi menu, East and West.

2 sheets sushi nori
½ avocado, pitted, peeled and sliced
1 tbs. fresh lemon juice
1 cup cooked sushi rice, page 13
½ cucumber, peeled, seeded and sliced
¼ lb. fresh crabmeat
wasabi as an accompaniment
soy sauce as an accompaniment
pickled ginger as an accompaniment
black sesame seeds for garnish

Heat nori in 350° oven to soften slightly, about 3 to 4 minutes. Rub avocado with lemon juice. Working with one sheet of nori at a time, with shiny side facing down and with a long side facing you, spread about ½ cup of the rice in an even layer on each sheet, leaving a ½-inch border on the long sides. Arrange some avocado strips horizontally across middle of rice, followed by a layer of cucumber and crab. Dab crab meat with wasabi. Follow rolling procedure on page 5. Cut into 6 equal slices and sprinkle generously with sesame seeds. Makes 12 slices.

ENGLISH CUCUMBER ROLL (KAPPA)

A staple vegetarian item, this roll is always a must when ordering from the sushi bar. English cucumbers work best because their size allows for long, manageable strips.

2 pieces sushi nori
1 cup cooked sushi rice, page 13
¼ cup plum paste
½ cucumber, peeled and cut into ½-inch strips

Heat nori in a 350° oven to soften slightly, about 3 to 4 minutes. Working with one sheet of nori at a time, with shiny side facing down and with long side facing you, spread ½ cup of the rice in an even layer on each sheet, leaving a ½-inch border on long sides. Spread a thin layer of plum paste across rice. Arrange a line of cucumber across middle of rice. Follow rolling procedure on page 5 and cut into 6 equal slices. Makes 12 slices.

SPICY TUNA ROLL (TEKA MAKI)

Tuna rolls are the ultimate in sushi rolls. This one is kicked up a notch with some hot chili sauce.

2 pieces sushi nori
1 cup cooked sushi rice, page 13
1/4 lb. fresh ahi tuna, cut into 1/2-inch wide strips
1 tbs. chili sauce
1 tbs. white sesame seeds, plus more for sprinkling
2 green onions, ends trimmed

Heat nori in a 350° oven to soften. Working with one sheet of nori at a time, with shiny side facing down and with long side facing you, spread 1/2 cup of the rice in an even layer on each sheet, leaving a 1/2-inch border on long sides. Arrange a line of tuna across middle of rice. Brush with chili sauce and sprinkle with sesame seeds. Place green onion on top of tuna. Follow rolling procedure on page 5 and cut each roll into 6 equal slices. Sprinkle with sesame seeds. Makes 12 slices.

EGGS McSUSHI ROLL
(TAMAGO)

For those on-the-go fast-food eaters, "have this your way" on the way to work. There won't be a wait at the drive-through, either!

1 tbs. canola cooking oil
½ carrot, peeled and cut into ½-inch strips
1 clove garlic, mashed
1 slice fresh ginger, mashed
1 tsp. rice vinegar
1 tbs. soy sauce
2 eggs
2 pieces sushi nori
1 cup cooked sushi rice, page 13
2 tbs. plum paste
2 green onions, ends trimmed

In a small skillet over medium-high heat, heat oil. Sauté carrot, garlic and ginger about 2 minutes, or until carrots are tender-crisp. In a small bowl, whisk rice vinegar, soy sauce and eggs. Add to skillet and cook until eggs are firm. Cut omelet into ½-inch wide strips. Heat nori. Working with one sheet of nori at a time, with shiny side facing down and with long side facing you, spread ½ cup of the rice in an even layer on each sheet, leaving a ½-inch border on long sides. Brush middle of rice with plum paste. Place omelet strips in a line across middle of rice. Follow rolling procedure on page 5 and cut each roll into 6 equal slices. Makes 12 slices.

PORTOBELLO ROLL

Portobello mushrooms are thick, rich in taste and are a beautiful deep brown color. You might think you are eating eel.

2 pieces sushi nori
1 tbs. butter
2 medium-sized portobello mushroom,
wiped clean, stems removed and coarsely chopped
1 cup cooked sushi rice, page 13

Heat nori in a 350° oven to soften, about 3 to 4 minutes. In a sauté pan over medium-high heat, heat butter. Sauté mushrooms until tender, about 3 to 4 minutes. Working with one sheet of nori at a time, with shiny side facing down and with long side facing you, spread ½ cup of the rice in an even layer on each sheet, leaving a ½-inch border on long sides. Spoon equal amounts of mushrooms in a line across middle of rice. Follow rolling procedure on page 5 and cut each roll into 6 equal slices. Makes 2 rolls.

SALMON SUSHI
(SHAKE MAKI)

The ideal time to make this sushi is when the salmon just start their spring run in mid-May.

2 cups water
2 tbs. vinegar
1 small salmon fillet (¼ lb.)
salt and pepper to taste

2 sheets sushi nori
1 cup cooked sushi rice, page 13
2 green onions, ends trimmed

Place salmon fillet in a dish and coat with vinegar and salt; cover with plastic wrap. Marinate until cured, about 3 hours; discard marinade. Break salmon into small chunks. Working with one sheet of nori at a time, with shiny side facing down and with long side facing you, spread ½ cup of the rice in a layer on each sheet, leaving a ½-inch border on long sides. Place salmon strips in a line across middle of rice. Place green onions on top of salmon. Follow rolling procedure on page 5. Cut into 6 equal slices. Makes 12 slices.

POACHED SALMON SUSHI

For those "fraidy cats" who love salmon, but may be too timid to swallow the raw stuff, poaching preserves its subtle texture.

1 small salmon fillet (¼ lb.)
¼ cup vinegar
2 tbs. salt
1 cup water
2 sheets sushi nori

1 cup cooked sushi rice, page 13
salt and pepper to taste
2 tbs. salt
2 green onions, ends trimmed

In a shallow pan, bring water and vinegar to a boil. Reduce heat to a simmer. Add salmon and cook for about 4 minutes. Remove from water and break into chunks; cool and season with salt and pepper. Heat nori. Working with one sheet of nori at a time, with shiny side facing down and with long side facing you, spread ½ cup of the rice in an even layer on each sheet, leaving a ½-inch border on long sides. Place salmon in a line across middle of rice. Place a green onion in each roll. Follow rolling procedure on page 5 and cut each roll into 6 equal slices. Makes 12 slices.

EEL ROLL (UNAGI)

Pick up prebarbecued eel at a local Japanese market or buy a few pieces from the local sushi bar. The time you save is worth the small price.

2 sheets sushi nori
1 cup cooked sushi rice, page 13
¼ lb. barbecued eel
½ avocado, pitted, peeled and cut into ½-inch slices

Heat nori. Working with one sheet of nori at a time, with shiny-side facing down and with long side facing you, spread ½ cup of the rice in an even layer on each sheet, leaving a ½-inch border on the long sides. Place eel in a horizontal line across middle of rice. Place avocado strips in a layer on top of eel. Follow rolling procedure on page 5 and cut each roll into 6 equal slices. Makes 12 slices.

CRAB AND EDAMAME BEAN ROLL

Edamame beans are fresh green Japanese soy beans.

2 sheets sushi nori
1 cup cooked sushi rice, page 13
4 oz. fresh crabmeat
½ cup boiled, shelled edamame beans

Heat nori. Working with one sheet of nori at a time, with shiny side facing down and with long side facing you, spread rice in an even layer on each sheet, leaving a ½-inch border on long sides. Line equal amounts of crabmeat in center of each roll. Top with a layer of edamame beans. Follow rolling procedure on page 5 and cut each roll into 6 equal slices. Makes 12 slices.

Variations:

• Add ¼ cup mayonnaise on top of crab layer.

• Add precooked baby shrimp on top of crab layer.

• Spread 2 oz. whipped cream cheese on rice; top with crab.

TOBIKO ROLL

Tobiko, or flying fish roe, means fish eggs. This specialty is commonly found in Japanese markets. Make this an inside-out roll and dab with enough tobiko to cover.

2 sheets sushi nori
1 cup cooked sushi rice, page 13
¼ lb. salmon skin
¼ cup tobiko

Heat nori. Working with one sheet of nori at a time, with shiny side facing down and with long side facing you, spread rice in an even layer on each sheet, leaving a ½-inch border on long sides. Line equal amounts of salmon skin in center of each roll. Follow inside-out rolling procedure on page 5 and cut each roll into 6 equal pieces. Dab with tobiko. Makes 12 slices.

THE MIDTOWN ROLL
(THE NEW YORK ROLL)

New Yorkers will forever be bonded to lox and cream cheese. Mid-town Manhattan is teaming with delis and bagel shops. This roll was created for those devotees.

2 sheets sushi nori
1 cup cooked sushi rice, page 13
½ cucumber, peeled, seeded and cut in ½-inch slices
¼ cup whipped cream cheese
¼ lb. smoked salmon

Working with one sheet of nori, with shiny side facing down and with long side facing you, spread ½ cup rice in an even layer on each sheet, leaving a ½-inch border on long sides. Place cucumber in a horizontal line across middle of rice. Spread cream cheese on top of cucumber strips in a thin layer. Place smoked salmon on top of cream cheese. Follow rolling procedure on page 5 and cut each roll into 12 equal slices.

PLANTAIN AND SHRIMP ROLL

Plaintains are staple items of Carribean cooking.

1 ripe plantain, peeled and cut into ½-inch slices
2 tbs. canola oil
6 large tiger shrimp, peeled and deveined
2 sheets sushi nori
1 cup cooked sushi rice, page 13

Heat oven to 375°. Arrange plantain on a baking sheet and bake for 10 minutes, or until very soft. Set aside to cool.

In a small skillet over medium heat, heat oil and add shrimp. Toss until shrimp turn white; remove and cool. When cool, chop coarsely. Heat nori. Working with one sheet of nori at a time, with shiny side facing down and with long side facing you, spread ½ cup of the rice in an even layer on each sheet, leaving a ½-inch border on long sides. Layer equal amounts of plantain slices in center of each roll. Arrange shrimp over plantains. Follow rolling procedure on page 5 and cut each roll into 6 equal slices. Makes 12 slices.

SHRIMP AND PINEAPPLE ROLL

If you are one who appreciates the tart, stinging flavor of pineapple, this roll is for you! Forget about putting pineapple on your pizza, try using it here, instead.

2 tbs. canola oil
6 black tiger shrimp, peeled and deveined
½ cup cooked sushi rice, page 13
2 sheets sushi nori
½ cup fresh pineapple chunks

Score shrimp across backs and press down to elongate. In a small skillet over medium-high heat, heat oil. Add shrimp and cook until white. Remove from heat and cool. Chop coarsely.

Heat nori. Working with one sheet of nori at a time, with shiny side facing down and with long side facing you, spread ½ cup of the rice in an even layer on each sheet, leaving a ½-inch border on long sides. Spoon equal amounts of shrimp in a line across middle of rice. Top with a layer of pineapple. Follow rolling procedure on page 5 and cut into 6 equal slices. Makes 12 slices.

THE (310) ROLL

Michael McCarty, a founding father of "California cuisine", is known for his innovative cooking style. This roll pays tribute to the Santa Monica pioneer who started the trend.

2 sheets sushi nori
1 avocado, peeled and pitted
1 tbs. lemon juice
1 cup cooked sushi rice, page 13
1 tbs. plum sauce
1 cup English peas, shelled, cooked in boiling water until
tender and refreshed in cold water
1 mango, pitted, peeled and cut
into ½-inch wide strips

Heat nori in a 350° oven to soften, about 3 to 4 minutes. Cut avocado into ½-inch strips and rub with lemon juice. Working with 1 sheet of nori at a time, shiny side facing down and long side facing you, spread ½ cup of the rice in an even layer on each sheet, leaving a ½-inch border on long sides. Brush plum sauce in a line across middle of rice. Arrange equal amounts of English peas and sliced mango on top of plum sauce. Top with a layer of avocado. Follow rolling procedure on page 5 and cut each roll into 6 equal slices. Makes 12 slices.

SWEET POTATO SUSHI

The Japanese sometimes grate raw sweet potatoes over their food for garnish. Cooked, the heavy, sweet flesh makes a smooth filling.

2 sheets cooked sushi nori
1 cup sushi rice, page 13
1 small cooked Jersey sweet potato,
peeled and sliced into ½-inch strips
¼ cup plum sauce

Heat nori. Working with one sheet of nori at a time, with shiny side facing down and with long side facing you, spread ½ cup of the rice in an even layer on each sheet, leaving a ½-inch border on long sides. Place equal amounts of sweet potato in a line across middle of rice. Brush each with 2 tbs. plum sauce. Follow rolling procedure on page 5 and cut each roll into 6 equal slices. Makes 12 slices.

ANCHOVY AND SUN-DRIED TOMATO SUSHI

Never mind making a trek to the local fish market; pick up a tin of anchovies and roll these up instead!

2 sheets sushi nori
1 cup cooked sushi rice
1 can (3.5 oz.) anchovies, drained
6 sun-dried tomatoes, wiped dry

Heat nori. Working with one sheet of nori at a time, with shiny side facing down and with long side facing you, spread ½ cup of the rice in an even layer on each sheet, leaving a ½-inch border on long sides. Arrange equal amounts of anchovies in a line across middle of rice. Place tomatoes in a layer on top of anchovies. Follow rolling procedure on page 5 and cut each roll into 6 equal slices. Makes 12 slices.

ISLAND SHRIMP SUSHI ROLL

The grated coconut gives these shrimp a taste of the islands.
It also offers a little sweetness, waking up the flavor of the shrimp.

6 large black tiger shrimp, peeled and deveined
1 tbs. olive oil
¼ cup grated coconut
¼ tsp. ground ginger
1 tsp. lemon juice
salt and pepper to taste
2 sheets sushi nori
1 cup cooked sushi rice, page 13

Score shrimp across backs and press down to elongate. In a small skillet over medium-high heat, heat oil. Add shrimp, coconut, ginger, lemon juice, salt and pepper and continue cooking until heated through. Remove from heat and cool. When cool, chop coarsely. Heat nori. Working with one sheet of nori at a time, with shiny side facing down and with long side facing you, spread ½ cup of the rice in an even layer on each sheet, leaving a ½-inch border on long sides. Arrange equal amounts of shrimp in a line across middle of rice. Follow rolling procedure on page 5 and cut each roll into 6 equal slices. Makes 12 slices.

GOAT CHEESE, CORN AND BASIL ROLL

These roll ingredients originated from a tamale filling, but they go just as well wrapped tightly in a sushi roll!

2 sheets sushi nori
1 cup cooked sushi rice, page 13
4 oz. fresh goat cheese
½ cup cooked corn kernels
¼ cup minced fresh basil leaves

Heat nori. Working with one sheet of nori at a time, with shiny side facing down and with long side facing you, spread ½ cup of the rice in an even layer on each sheet, leaving a ½-inch border on long sides. Spread goat cheese in equal amounts in a line across middle of rice. Layer with corn and basil leaves. Follow rolling method on page 5 and cut each roll into 6 equal slices. Makes 12 slices.

GINGER SCALLOP ROLL

Asian flavors come alive in a refreshing and simple roll.

2 tbs. butter
24 bay scallops
2 tbs. chopped fresh ginger
2 tbs. chopped fresh cilantro
2 sheets sushi nori
1 cup cooked sushi rice, page 13

In a small skillet over medium heat, melt butter. Add scallops, ginger and cilantro and cook 4 minutes, until scallops are golden brown. Remove from heat and cool. heat nori. Working with one sheet of nori at a time, with shiny side facing down and with long side facing you, spread ½ cup of the rice in an even layer on each sheet, leaving a ½-inch border on long sides. Place equal amounts of scallops, 12 on each sheet, in a line across middle of rice. Folllow rolling procedure on page 5 and cut each roll into 6 equal slices. Makes 12 slices.

SEARED OYSTER ROLL

This roll certainly might improve your chance for romance.

2 tbs. butter
2 shallots, minced
12 oysters in half shell, shells removed
pepper to taste
2 sheets sushi nori
1 cup cooked sushi rice. page 13
1 cup torn arugula leaves

In a small skillet over medium heat, heat butter. Add shallots and oysters and sear for 10 seconds on each side. Season with pepper and remove; let cool.

Heat nori. Working with one sheet of nori at a time, with shiny side facing down and with long side facing you, spread ½ cup of the rice in an even layer on each sheet, leaving a ½-inch border on long sides. Arrange oysters in a line across middle of rice. Top with arugula leaves. Follow rolling procedure on page 5 and cut each roll into 6 equal slices. Makes 12 slices.

MUSSEL SHOALS SUSHI ROLL

Hazy Southern California coastline is where you can pick up a little mussel – of both kinds! And if you eat your spinach, you're likely to get some.

2 sheets sushi nori
1 cup cooked sushi rice, page 13
12 cooked green lip mussels, shelled
1 cup baby spinach leaves

Heat nori. Working with one sheet of nori at a time, with shiny side facing down and with long side facing you, spread rice in a layer on each sheet, leaving a ½-inch border on long sides. Place equal amounts of mussels, 6 on each sheet, in a line across middle of rice. Top with spinach leaves. Folllow rolling procedure on page 5 and cut each roll into 6 equal slices. Makes 12 slices.

MOROCCAN ROLL

These flavors may inspire a further look into the foods of the dark and mysterious continent of Africa.

½ cup shredded zucchini
½ cup shredded red cabbage
1 jalapeño pepper, seeded and minced
1 clove garlic, minced
1 tsp. ground cumin
salt and pepper to taste
1 tbs. olive oil
2 sheets sushi nori
1 cup cooked sushi rice, page 13
¼ cup toasted pine nuts

In a large skillet over medium heat, sauté zucchini, cabbage, jalapeño, garlic and spices in oil until vegetables are soft. With a slotted spoon, remove zucchini mixture and transfer to a small bowl; let cool. Heat nori. Working with one sheet of nori at a time, with shiny side facing down and with long side facing you, spread rice in a layer on sheet on each sheet, leaving a ½-inch border on long sides. Place equal amounts of zucchini mixture in center of each roll. Sprinkle with pine nuts. Follow rolling procedure on page 5 and cut each roll into 6 equal slices. Makes 12 slices.

SMOKED SALMON AND FIG ROLL

April and May mean open season on salmon and a time when fresh figs are falling from orchard trees.

2 sheets sushi nori
1 cup cooked sushi rice, page 13
4 oz. piece smoked salmon, broken into small pieces
2 mission figs, thinly sliced

Working with 1 sheet of nori at a time, shiny side facing down and long side facing you, spread rice in an even layer on each nori sheet, leaving a ½-inch border on long sides. Arrange salmon in a line across middle of rice. Top with a layer of figs. Follow rolling procedure on page 5 and cut into 6 equal slices. Makes 12 slices.

Variation

Prosciutto and Fig Roll: Add 2 very thin slices of prosciutto on each sheet instead of salmon and top with a layer of figs.

SMOKED SALMON AND MANGO ROLL

The sweet fruit flavors, often times, are overlooked as perfectly suitable complements to savory items. Mango, like salmon, is fleshy and a substantial match.

2 sheets sushi nori
1 cup cooked sushi rice, page 13
4 oz. chunk smoked salmon, broken into small pieces
1 mango, pitted, peeled and cut
into ½-inch wide strips

Heat nori. Working with 1 sheet of nori at a time, shiny side facing down and long side facing you, spread ½ cup of the rice in an even layer on each nori sheet, leaving a ½-inch border on long sides. Arrange equal amounts of salmon in a line across middle of rice. Top with a layer of mango. Follow rolling procedure on page 5 and cut into 6 equal slices. Makes 12 slices.

TUNA FISH ROLL

When time is of the essence and you need a quick fix, this roll is an easy out.

2 sheets sushi nori
1 cup cooked sushi rice, page 13
¼ cup mayonnaise
1 can albacore tuna in water, drained
pepper to taste

Heat nori. Working with one sheet of nori at a time, with shiny side facing down and with long side facing you, spread ½ cup of the rice in an even layer on each sheet, leaving a ½-inch border on long sides. Spread mayonnaise in a line across middle of rice. Top with tuna. Season with pepper and follow rolling procedure on page 5. Cut each roll into 6 equal slices. Makes 12 slices.

Variation: Northern Italian Tuna Roll

Add ¼ cup cannelini beans on top of tuna and sprinkle with 1 tbs. rosemary.

SUSHI – THE NEW SCHOOL

SCALLOP AND
AVOCADO SUSHI ROLL

The light flavor of scallops balances its heavier partner, the avocado.

¼ lb. bay scallops
¼ cup lime juice
½ avocado, pitted, peeled and cut into ½-inch slices
1 cup cooked sushi rice, page 13
2 sheets sushi nori

In a bowl, combine scallops with lime juice. Cover with plastic wrap and set aside for 15 minutes. Heat nori. Working with one sheet of nori at a time, with shiny side facing down and with long side facing you, spread ½ cup of the rice in an even layer on each sheet, leaving a ½-inch border on long sides. Line equal amounts of scallops across middle of rice. Top with a layer of avocado. Follow rolling procedure on page 5 and cut each roll into 6 equal slices. Makes 12 slices.

Variation

Arrange a layer of cooked calamari on top of avocado.

PROSCIUTTO AND CANTALOUPE ROLL

Prosciutto is the ham of choice to use. If you can't find it, look for a good dry, cured local ham for this roll.

2 sheets sushi nori
1 cup cooked sushi rice, page 13
6 very thin slices prosciutto
½ cup thinly sliced cantaloupe

Heat nori. Working with one sheet of nori at a time, with shiny side facing down and with long side facing you, spread ½ cup rice in an even layer on each sheet, leaving a ½-inch border on long sides. Line each roll with equal amounts of prosciutto, 3 slices, across rice. Lay a layer of cantaloupe slices across middle of rice. Follow rolling procedure on page 5 and cut each roll into 6 equal slices. Makes 12 slices.

A VERY "DUCKY" ROLL

Pick up some precooked barbecued duck from a Chinese market or from the deli counter at a specialty foods store.

2 sheets sushi nori
1 cup cooked sushi rice, page 13
1 cup chopped Chinese barbecue duck
12 basil leaves

Heat nori. Working with 1 sheet of nori at a time, shiny side facing down and long side facing you, spread rice ½ cup of the rice in an even layer on each nori sheet, leaving a ½-inch border on long sides. Arrange duck in a line across middle of rice. Top with basil leaves. Follow rolling procedure on page 5 and cut into 6 even slices. Makes 12 slices.

JAPANESE EGGPLANT SUSHI

This roll has a smooth and rich filling. Eggplant and nori are perfect partners.

1 small Japanese eggplant
salt to taste
1 tbs. canola oil
1 cup cooked sushi rice, page 13
2 sheets sushi nori

Cut eggplant into ½-inch strips. Place in colander and sprinkle with salt. Let stand for 15 minutes. In a small skillet over medium heat, heat oil and cook eggplant strips for 20 minutes, or until completely cooked. Remove from heat and cool. Heat nori. Working with one sheet of nori at a time, with shiny side facing down and with long side facing you, spread ½ cup of the rice in an even layer on each sheet, leaving a ½-inch border on long sides. Place equal amounts of eggplant in a line across middle of rice. Follow rolling procedure on page 5 and cut each roll into 6 equal slices. Makes 12 slices.

THE STEAK ROLL

For the carnivores who must have their meat, this sushi roll will steer you in the right direction.

¼ lb. boneless sirloin steak, ½-inch thick, trimmed
salt and pepper to taste
2 sheets sushi nori
1 cup cooked sushi rice, page 13
2 green onions, ends trimmed

Prepare a very hot barbecue. Grill steak for 3 to 4 minutes on both sides until browned. Do not overcook; steak is very thin. Season with salt and pepper, let cool and slice into thin strips.

Heat nori. Working with one sheet of nori at a time, with shiny side facing down and with long side facing you, spread ½ cup rice in an even layer on each sheet, leaving a ½-inch border on long sides. Place equal amounts of steak slices in a line across middle of rice. Top each with a green onion. Follow rolling procedure on page 5 and cut each roll into 6 equal slices. Makes 12 slices.

THE GREEN ROLL

Sneak your daily serving of leafy greens into a roll!

½ bunch collard greens or any other dark, green leafy vegetable
2 tbs. olive oil
1 clove garlic, minced
salt and pepper to taste
2 sheets sushi nori
½ cup cooked sushi rice, page 13
black sesame seeds for garnish

In a medium-sized skillet over medium heat, sauté greens in oil and garlic for about 5 minutes, or until bright, but tender. Drain greens well on a layer of paper towels. Season with salt and pepper. Heat nori. Working with one sheet of nori at a time, with shiny side facing down and with long side facing you, spread ½ cup of the rice in a layer on each sheet, leaving a ½-inch border on long sides. Place equal amounts of greens in center of each roll, folllow rolling procedure on page 5 and cut roll into 6 equal slices. Sprinkle with black sesame seeds. Makes 12 slices.

SPRING ROLL

This filling was inspired by Thai rice paper rolls. A cucumber salad or a Thai peanut sauce are perfect accompaniments.

2 sheets sushi nori
1 cup cooked sushi rice, page 13
½ cup snow peas
½ cup shredded carrot
½ cup enoki mushrooms
1/4 cup fresh mint leaves
1/4 cup fresh Thai basil leaves
4 tbs. chili sauce

Heat nori. Working with 1 sheet of nori at a time, with shiny side facing down and long side facing you, spread ½ cup of the rice in an even layer on each nori sheet, leaving a ½-inch border on long sides. Place equal amounts of snow peas in a line across middle of rice. Add a layer of carrot, mushrooms, mint and basil. Spread 2 tbs. chili sauce on each roll. Follow rolling method on page 5 and cut into 6 equal slices. Makes 12 slices.

BLACKENED CATFISH ROLL

This roll has a little Cajun flavor jam-packed in for a punch.

2 tbs. butter
¼ lb. freshwater catfish fillet
cayenne pepper to taste
2 sheets sushi nori
1 cup cooked sushi rice, page 13
½ cup red beans

In a small skillet over medium-high heat, melt butter. Add catfish, sprinkle generously with cayenne and cook for 2 to 3 minutes on each side until blackened. Remove from skillet and cool; break into bite-size pieces. Heat nori. Working with one sheet of nori at a time, with shiny side facing down and with long side facing you, spread ½ cup of the rice in a layer on each sheet, leaving a ½-inch border on long sides. Arrange equal amounts of catfish pieces in a line across middle of rice. Top with a layer of red beans. Follow rolling procedure on page 4 and cut each roll into 6 equal slices. Makes 12 slices.

TOMATO AND CUCUMBER ROLL

This refreshing roll makes a great palate cleanser.

1 tomato, seeded, diced and strained
½ cup peeled, seeded, diced cucumber
1 tbs. rice wine vinegar
2 tbs. chopped fresh flat-leaf parsley
2 tsp. sugar
salt and pepper to taste
2 sheets sushi nori
1 cup cooked sushi rice, page 13

In a bowl, combine tomato and cucumber with vinegar, parsley, sugar, salt and pepper; mix well. Cover and chill. Working with one sheet of nori at a time, with shiny side facing down and with long side facing you, spread ½ cup of the rice in a layer on each sheet, leaving a ½-inch border on long sides. Place equal amounts of tomato mixture in a line across middle of each roll. Follow rolling procedure on page 5 and cut each roll into 6 equal slices. Makes 12 slices.

TROUT ALMONDINE ROLL

A classic preparation that defined the cosmopolitan dining era of the late 1960s is resurrected and takes on a new look here.

¼ cup butter
¼ lb. trout fillet
2 tbs. sweet vermouth
salt and pepper to taste
½ cup sliced, almonds, toasted
2 sheets sushi nori
1 cup cooked sushi rice, page 13

In a small skillet over medium-high heat, melt butter. Add fillet to skillet, pour in vermouth and cook for 2 to 3 minutes on each side, or until lightly browned. Season with salt and pepper. Remove from skillet, let cool and break into pieces. Heat nori. Working with one sheet of nori at a time, with shiny side facing down and with long side facing you, spread ½ cup of the rice in an even layer on each sheet, leaving a ½-inch border on long sides. Place trout in a line across middle of rice. Top with almonds. Follow rolling procedure on page 5 and cut each roll into 6 equal slices. Makes 12 slices.

BLT ROLL

All of the lunchbox sandwich elements are present and accounted for, except for the bread. The sushi rice provides the perfect holder for this addicting combination.

2 sheets sushi nori
1 cup cooked sushi rice, page 13
¼ cup mayonnaise
4 slices cooked bacon
2 large iceberg lettuce leaves
1 Roma tomato, thinly sliced

Heat nori. Working with one sheet of nori at a time, with shiny side facing down and with long side facing you, spread ½ cup of the rice in a layer on each sheet, leaving a ½-inch border on long sides. Spread each sheet with a layer of mayonnaise. Top with a layer of lettuce. Place equal amounts of bacon, 2 slices per sheet, across middle of rice and top with a layer of tomato. Folllow rolling procedure on page 5 and cut each roll into 6 equal slices. Makes 12 slices.

GRILLED FIG ROLL

The intense fig flavors are captured. This can be served as an appetizer or a dessert.

6 small fresh mission figs, sliced
2 tbs. port
2 tbs. sugar
2 sheets sushi nori
1 cup cooked sushi rice, page 13

Heat broiler. Place figs on a baking sheet, flesh side up. Brush figs with port and sprinkle with sugar. Broil for 2 to 3 minutes, or until figs are golden. Remove from oven and let cool. Heat nori. Working with one sheet of nori at a time, with shiny side facing down and with long side facing you, spread ½ cup of the rice in a layer on each sheet, leaving a ½-inch border on long sides. Place equal amounts of fig slices in a line across middle of rice. Follow rolling procedure on page 5 and cut each roll into 6 equal slices. Makes 12 slices.

NECTARINE ROLL

For this roll, use nectarines that are firm. Overly ripe fruit makes the roll difficult to handle.

2 sheets sushi nori
1 cup cooked sushi rice, page 13
2 small nectarines, pitted and thinly sliced
½ cup torn arugula leaves

Heat nori. Working with one sheet of nori at a time, with shiny side facing down and with long side facing you, spread ½ cup of the rice in a layer on each sheet, leaving a ½-inch border on long sides. Place equal amounts of nectarine slices in a line across middle of rice. Top with arugula leaves. Follow rolling procedure on page 5 and cut each roll into 6 equal slices. Makes 12 slices.

APRICOT AND ALMOND ROLL

If you don't have Sauternes in the pantry, sherry or port will do.

6 small apricots, pitted, peeled and sliced
2 tbs. Sauternes or other sweet dessert wine
2 tbs. sugar
¼ cup sliced almonds, toasted
2 sheets sushi nori
1 cup cooked sushi rice, page 13

Heat broiler. Place apricots on a baking sheet. Brush with Sauternes and sprinkle with sugar. Broil for 1 to 2 minutes, or until sugar dissolves. Remove from oven and let cool. Heat nori. Working with one sheet of nori at a time, with shiny side facing down and with long side facing you, spread ½ cup of the rice in a layer on each sheet, leaving a ½-inch border on long sides. Place equal amounts of apricots in a line across middle of rice. Top with sliced almonds. Follow rolling procedure on page 5 and cut each roll into 6 equal slices. Makes 12 slices.

THE PEANUT BUTTER AND JELLY ROLL

This one is for the PB&J devotees. Who says you need spongy white bread when you've got sushi rice to hold it the goo?

2 sheets sushi nori
1 cup cooked sushi rice, page 13
½ cup chunky peanut butter
¼ cup raspberry jam

Heat nori. Working with one sheet of nori at a time, with shiny side facing down and long side facing you, spread rice in an even layer on each sheet, leaving a ½-inch border on long sides. Spread equal amounts of peanut butter across middle of rice. Wet knife and spread a layer of jam on top of peanut butter. Follow rolling method on page 5 and cut into 6 equal slices. Makes 12 slices.

Variation

Peanut Butter-Banana Roll: Spread layer of peanut butter across rice. Layer with banana slices.

NUTELLA ROLL

Nutella, the chocolate and hazelnut spread, has become increasingly common in the United States. It is often found next to the peanut butter in your supermarket. You may have a little trouble keeping the filling intact, but this roll will disappear so quickly that its appearance will hardly be noticed.

2 sheets sushi nori
1 cup cooked sushi rice, page 13
½ cup Nutella

Heat nori. Working with one sheet of nori at a time, with shiny side facing down and with long side facing you, spread ½ cup rice in a layer on each sheet, leaving a ½-inch border on long sides. Spread equal amounts of Nutella in a line across middle of rice. Follow rolling procedure on page 5 and cut each roll into 6 equal slices. Makes 2 slices.

_____
_____
_____
_____
_____
_____
_____
_____
_____
_____

MY SUSHI ROLLS

_____
_____
_____
_____
_____
_____
_____
_____
_____
_____

MY SUSHI ROLLS

_____

_____

_____

_____

_____

_____

_____

_____

_____

_____

MY SUSHI ROLLS

_____

_____

_____

_____

_____

_____

_____

_____

_____

_____

MY SUSHI ROLLS

_____
_____
_____
_____
_____
_____
_____
_____
_____
_____

MY SUSHI ROLLS

_____
_____
_____
_____
_____
_____
_____
_____
_____
_____

MY SUSHI ROLLS

MY SUSHI ROLLS

_____
_____
_____
_____
_____
_____
_____
_____
_____
_____

MY SUSHI ROLLS

_____

_____

_____

_____

_____

_____

_____

_____

_____

_____

MY SUSHI ROLLS

SELECTED BIBLIOGRAPHY

- About Wasabi. http://freshwasabi.com/about.html
- Epicurious Recipe File.
http://food.epicurious.com/db/recipes/recipesH/9/6009.html
- International Sushi Maker Plus.
http://www.sushimaker.com/main.html
- Michael's. http://www.w2.com/docs2/act/food/michaels/bio.html
- Salt Spring Sushi Page. http://www.saltspring.com/sush
- Sushi Central. http:// www.lynx.com/pje/sush.html
- Sushi! Sushi! Sushi. http://catalog.com/sush
- Sushi World Guide. http://www.sushi.infogate.de/linx.htm#2
- Tampa Bay Sushi Society.
http://www.mesams.org/sushi/default.htm

THE FOLLOWING RESTAURANTS PROVIDED INSPIRATION:

Chopsticks Cafe. Pacific Grove, California

Crazy Fish. Los Angeles, California

Draeger's Supermarket. San Mateo, California

Kamakura. Alameda, California

Kyoto. San Mateo, California

Robata Grill. Carmel, California

Sakae. Burlingame, California

Sho Gun Restaurant. San Leandro, California

Sushi on Main. Half Moon Bay, California

Wok-n-Roll. San Mateo, California

THANK YOU

INDEX